When I

Got Busy,
I Got
Better

AL-ANON FAMILY GROUPS®
hope for families & friends of alcoholics

The Al-Anon Family Groups are a fellowship of relatives and friends of alcoholics who share their experience, strength, and hope in order to solve their common problems. We believe alcoholism is a family illness and that changed attitudes can aid recovery.

Al-Anon is not allied with any sect, denomination, political entity, organization, or institution; does not engage in any controversy; neither endorses nor opposes any cause. There are no dues for membership. Al-Anon is self-supporting through its own voluntary contributions.

Al-Anon has but one purpose: to help families of alcoholics. We do this by practicing the Twelve Steps, by welcoming and giving comfort to families of alcoholics, and by giving understanding and encouragement to the alcoholic.

Suggested Preamble to the Twelve Steps

For information and catalog of literature write to
the World Service Office for Al-Anon and Alateen:

Al-Anon Family Group Headquarters, Inc.
1600 Corporate Landing Parkway
Virginia Beach, Virginia 23454-5617
757-563-1600   Fax 757-563-1655
Member site: www.al-anon.alateen.org/members
E-mail: wso@al-anon.org

Al-Anon/Alateen is supported by members' voluntary contributions and from the sale of our Conference Approved Literature.

 Approved by
World Service Conference
Al-Anon Family Groups

Table of Contents

Preamble

The Al-Anon Family Groups are a fellowship of relatives and friends of alcoholics who share their experience, strength, and hope in order to solve their common problems. We believe alcoholism is a family illness and that changed attitudes can aid recovery.

Al-Anon is not allied with any sect, denomination, political entity, organization, or institution; does not engage in any controversy; neither endorses nor opposes any cause. There are no dues for membership. Al-Anon is self-supporting through its own voluntary contributions.

Al-Anon has but one purpose: to help families of alcoholics. We do this by practicing the Twelve Steps, by welcoming and giving comfort to families of alcoholics, and by giving understanding and encouragement to the alcoholic.

Suggested Preamble to the Twelve Steps

Facing
Our Fears

Al-Anon service?

When I first consider reaching out to others, I might hesitate: Didn't I come to Al-Anon to focus on my individual experience, to seek my own recovery? Wouldn't contributing to the common good just divert me from personal progress? After finally learning to focus on myself, wouldn't helping others distract me from that goal?

It's true that Al-Anon is a personal program, that it encourages us to face our own particular circumstances. But it is also a program in which each member's recovery is based on a common sharing of experience, strength, and hope. The Twelve Steps helps us to heal as individuals, but they also help us to heal our relationships and to work with others.

Practicing the Twelfth Step offers us an opportunity to share our program in a new way. We benefit when we practice gratitude, and Al-Anon service is gratitude in action. We acknowledge that we have made progress in recovery not on our own, but with the help of many others—and through the guidance of a Higher Power.

In helping others, we drop any pretense that *I alone* am in charge of *my* separate recovery. We acknowledge the common bond that unites us in the program, and we take steps (however halting and uneven) to align ourselves with the guidance of a Higher Power. By passing on the guidance we have received, we learn a new humility.

When we help those who want to be helped, we find new satisfaction in sharing the gift of recovery. We also find that the guidance of a Higher Power is an abundant resource on which we can draw again and again.

Service and recovery, then, are not independent of each other. Both are part of the spiritual awakening that continues to guide us. The more willing we become to practice all of this program, the more progress we can make in recovering from the effects of another's alcoholism and in living our lives more fully.

Still, we might find the concept of doing service daunting, difficult, or frightening. The word itself has as much appeal as "duty," "responsibility," "commitment," or "work." We come to Al-Anon in various stages of desperation, confusion, and distrust—and before we know it, we are hearing about hastening our recovery not just by sharing in meetings but by participating in group affairs.

The tasks suggested may not be difficult or demanding, but we might nonetheless be daunted at the mere thought of lending a hand. We've been described (before coming to Al-Anon) as people who, forgetting that we ourselves can't swim, would jump in the water to save someone who's drowning. No wonder, then, if we are unwilling to get our feet wet when it comes to a commitment to help out! Experience with alcoholism has left many of us afraid to get involved, lest we be hurt by our own efforts.

The thought of participating in any activity may call up our worst fears of experiencing all over again the criticism, embarrassment, frustration, and even despair we have known in the past. Our attempts to help others grapple with the disease of alcoholism might bring us face to face again with the loss of the illusion of control that can result from lending a hand.

What we may not notice, beyond our fears, is that Al-Anon

gives us a chance to do *just a little*—to fold a chair, to arrange literature on a table. At first we may experience some discomfort, but we can go at a pace that doesn't leave us overwhelmed. As we progress, we begin to notice the other side of service: We are learning and growing at an extraordinary pace.

Fear of Assuming Responsibility

I feared the prospect of chairing a meeting, of being in charge, of possibly having to deal with awkward situations or difficult people. But I agreed to try when a friend suggested I might be ready. It was a small group of Al-Anon members, and the meeting required little direction of any kind. Eventually, as my confidence grew, I was able to feel comfortable with even larger groups.

Looking back, I still recall my fears, but also remember the regular reassurance of more experienced members, who helped me to understand that I was no more in charge of a group than the next member: We all share equally in this responsibility. While I was not an expert in group dynamics or a skilled facilitator of group process, nobody expected me to have special skills or abilities, to be especially responsible or able—and I learned to accept the freedom this afforded me. The best I could do was good enough.

Fear of Making Mistakes

Could I manage to replenish coffee or literature supplies effectively without making the wrong choices? If I made a mistake, would others criticize me? Would I somehow damage our group through my error? I asked myself these questions before volunteering to serve coffee or take charge of the literature.

What I found through participation was that my group

viewed me as a trusted servant with the ability to listen to others and to respond to their needs and suggestions. I really did have permission to make choices—within the limits of my group's resources to fund them. Others accepted and appreciated my efforts, at whatever level I was able to contribute.

The freedom to make decisions, the appreciation of my efforts—both contrasted strongly with my earlier experience of dealing with alcoholism, and I gained a new self-acceptance. I learned to think of mistakes not as occasions for feeling shame but as invitations to make adjustments.

Fear of Making a Commitment

When I first came to Al-Anon, I appreciated the flexibility. I could come later, leave early, attend meetings anytime, and skip them anytime as well. Nobody needed to know my schedule. Nobody depended on me.

When I began to explore service opportunities, I was afraid of losing this flexibility and freedom. Would I feel trapped?

But I began to notice that service didn't destroy flexibility. I still had the support of the members of my group. If I couldn't keep a commitment, I could ask for help, and if I discovered a job was interfering with my life, I could step away without blame. I didn't get a report card or a job evaluation. In addition, my duties were always clearly defined and limited in duration. Nobody asked me to take on extra jobs or to extend my commitments.

To my surprise, my commitments gave me a chance to get better acquainted with the members of my group. I gained a new flexibility in my relationships with them, and a new freedom as my sense of acceptance grew. I often felt better after a meeting, whether I had really felt like attending or not, for I was welcomed no matter how I was feeling.

Fear of Failure

Sometimes responsibility brings up a fear more disconcerting than that of simply making mistakes: the fear of failure. What if I forget my story when it's my turn to share? What if I lose our literature, break our coffee pot, alienate my group, or lose our treasury? Alcoholism has given me a high level of creativity, when left to my own devices, to spin fantasies of disaster!

What I learned through Al-Anon service is that others want to see me succeed. Certainly my Higher Power is always with me and is always willing to encourage my success. My group, too, supports my efforts. I've also learned that the fate of my group doesn't rest in my hands, but rather in the hands of a Higher Power, who is *not* me. Help is always available.

Fear of Success

What if I volunteered to help out and succeeded? I didn't want to feel responsible for the welfare of my group.

What if I began to dominate the affairs of my group or became distracted from my own recovery by our deliberations about business?

And might I not lose a healthy sense of humility if people started looking to me for guidance?

My fear of success sprang from my experience with alcoholism and feeling that doing a job well meant sacrificing my own happiness. I discovered in Al-Anon that my fear of dominance was a good guarantee I wouldn't be domineering and that taking a hand in group affairs furthered my own recovery instead of derailing it.

I also discovered that I could grow in self-esteem without losing humility. I could enjoy making a contribution without feeling that I alone could provide guidance. Most important, in helping others, as in the rest of my program, Al-Anon urged me to let go. Part of extending a hand is eventually letting go and noticing that, when my job is done, there are more hands willing and able to carry on.

In Giving, We Receive

A friend tells about an experience that opened her eyes to Al-Anon's place in her life. One evening she sat debating whether to attend a meeting or stay home. The weather was bad, she felt tired, and she could think of projects that seemed pressing. At the moment she was deciding that perhaps she'd stay home, a thought about Al-Anon came to mind: *This is where hearts are healed.* That simple thought gave her the motivation necessary to set her own concerns aside and get to a meeting.

I think about my friend's story when I conduct my own debates about whether or not I can make the effort to get to a meeting. Sometimes, of course, my decision is easy: I really feel the need or I am simply following my plans for the day without second thoughts. Then again, there are days when my plans fall apart almost before I get out of bed.

One of the simple practices I've used over the years to sustain my willingness to attend meetings is making a commitment to perform one job related to the group, whether serving coffee, putting out literature, acting as Treasurer, or filling the position of Secretary. (Clearly, agreeing to speak at a meeting is also an excellent incentive for attendance!) In this way, I remove all debates about whether I have the time, the energy, or the willingness to attend by simply recognizing that I have a job to do. While performing my chosen task, I'm assured that I am part of a gathering where, however imperceptibly, hearts are being healed.

Many members find that Al-Anon service provides welcome, healing benefits.

A Reason to Keep Coming Back

When I first came to Al-Anon, I hoped, like many other people, to cure the alcoholic. I sat in meetings, listened attentively, and learned very quickly. Then I took all my newfound knowledge and left. I went home and told my husband that he was sick, that his problem wasn't mine, that I was going to have a life whether he was drinking or not. I'm sure someone at those meetings mentioned compassion, but I never heard it.

Months later, my husband somehow found his way into a rehab, and the professionals there suggested that I go to Al-Anon. "But why" I thought. "I already learned everything they had to teach me." Still, since I would do anything to help my man, I obediently returned to Al-Anon.

I attended a beginners' meeting, then regular meetings. Someone mentioned that sometimes newcomers took responsibility for making coffee. Determined to be the perfect Al-Anon member, I agreed to prepare coffee for the group, and I made a three-month commitment. So many nights when I wanted to stay home and take care of my husband, when I was afraid he might drink or not go to a meeting, when he was in a bad mood and I knew I could make it better, I didn't stay home—because I had made a commitment. Since I've always tried to keep commitments, I never missed a meeting.

I couldn't make a commitment to myself, but my first commitment to Al-Anon kept me coming back. I began to notice that the people in my group appeared happy and content. They seemed to deal with their problems in a different way. I knew that I wanted what they had, so I tried listening to them a sec-

ond time. This time my mind stopped racing. For one hour my focus shifted from the alcoholic, and I felt calm and peaceful. Eventually I was able to feel moments of peace outside the meeting. This was my first experience of growth through service.
I ask myself: What commitment am I willing to make?

A New View of Recovery

I can't begin to explain how big an impact really participating in my group has had on my recovery. When I first came to Al-Anon, all I wanted was for everyone to help me. I didn't want to know or need to know all that other stuff. I just wanted someone to show me how to keep the alcoholic from drinking.

Although I'd prefer not to admit it today, I once walked out of a meeting on the Traditions. How could hearing about such principles possibly help me? Needless to say, my opinions of the Traditions (and, indeed, many other tools of this program) have changed over the past 15 years.

After a few years in Al-Anon, I heard people say, "If your program seems stagnant, try service." I also heard them say, "Our Al-Anon triangle has three sides: Recovery through the Steps, Unity through the Traditions, and Service through the Concepts. If you aren't taking advantage of all three sides of this triangle, you may be cheating yourself."

I knew I didn't want to miss out on anything the fellowship had to offer, so I considered volunteering. I had to examine my motives carefully, because in my life prior to Al-Anon, low self-esteem had prompted me to volunteer for everything in the hope that others would like me.

Fortunately, I met a longtime Al-Anon member who instilled in me the desire to return something of what I had received. By volunteering for a service commitment, I could show my gratitude. What a joy to know that now my appreciation of others—not my lack of self-esteem—is my motivation!

Now that my current term of service as a Delegate is drawing to a close, part of me wants to rest and part of me knows that, when the occasion arises, I will help out again where needed. I'm forever grateful for the love I've received from all the members of Al-Anon.

I ask myself: How can I express my gratitude today?

Fellowship

Service was the last thing on my mind when I first attended Al-Anon. I felt so desperate and hopeless I could barely see beyond my own pain. But as I kept coming back, I began to notice people preparing coffee, setting out literature, arranging furniture. This activity all seemed natural and spontaneous: no prompting, no directing. People did what they did because they wanted to do it. After the meeting, I saw them again rearranging furniture, putting away literature, helping out. Most important, I saw people greeting me, extending a hand, smiling, sharing a hug.

At each meeting, I saw the same people doing the same things—but I also saw newcomers pitching in. I noticed, too, that members took turns chairing the meetings and that everyone shared in the reading of the Steps and Traditions. These small gestures suggested to me the depth of caring in fellowship.

I slowly started pitching in myself. Today I see how my small gestures gave me a sense of belonging and encouraged me to reach out to others. My actions led me to focus on something besides my own self-pity and resentment, and helped me embark on the road to recovery. When I began to feel good about myself, I could value my talents. The confidence others showed me was contagious. I came to believe that what I got from the program depended very much on what I gave.

Gradually I took on more responsibilities. I'm now a Group Representative, and this service has given me a special sense of caring for all the members of my group. Learning to take care of my responsibilities as a GR without taking on those of others has helped me in other situations and relationships. I've come to sense the miracle of a fellowship under "one authority: a loving God as He may express Himself in our group conscience." *I ask myself: What part can I play in this fellowship?*

Group Support

While many incidents in Al-Anon have had a tremendous impact on me, the most immediate and dramatic was my first time as a speaker at a meeting.

I wasn't sought out; I asked to speak. The week before my group's monthly speaker meeting, the Chairperson asked for volunteers. I got what I call a tap on the shoulder from my Higher Power, a sudden urge to respond. I've learned to trust these impulses, so I raised my hand.

The following week, I had the jitters, but not as badly as I'd feared. I'd been in Al-Anon quiet a while. I knew what to expect, but I had never imagined how powerful the experience would be.

My fears proved groundless. No one stalked out in disgust or muttered, "Couldn't they have found someone else?" I started to talk—about me—and they listened. No one interrupted or whispered to a neighbor or stood up to get coffee. No one told me to keep it short or cut me off for talking too long. No one said, "Can't you talk about anyone but yourself?"

They actually sat and listened with attention until I had finished talking. Throughout the break that followed, people approached me to thank me, to say how glad they were to hear me speak, to mention something I had said that had meaning for them, or to comment on a parallel in our two stories.

After the break, the meeting was opened for general discussion. Members shared what it was like to hear me speak, referring to parts of what I had said. I heard not one negative or even neutral response. Everything was positive and supportive—and it was all about *me*! I have never felt so valued.

None of this scenario was new, since I'd already attended many speaker meetings. The difference was where I sat in the group.

When I left the meeting, I felt as if I should weigh more than I had before. I felt more solid, more substantial, more real. It was the most validating experience I've ever had. It was as if I had, just then, become real.

I ask myself: Am I willing to share my story?

Replacing Isolation with Community

Recently I attended a neighborhood hearing to show support for a local service. To my surprise, I found myself taking part as an active and committed member of my community. My pre-Al-Anon feelings of isolation and frustration had abated as I established a connection with my neighbors.

In tracing the development of my new experience of common ground, I realized that my years in Al-Anon had been instrumental in dispelling my isolation. More specifically, I noticed that Al-Anon service had given me an experience of connection and commitment.

A member of our fellowship once explained how reaching out in simple ways had helped her break through her loneliness, desperation, and isolation. Straightening up after a meeting gave her the incentive she needed to overcome her fears and talk to other members. She let go of feeling invisible, fearful, and unworthy by focusing on the jobs that almost anyone can do, regardless of inner turmoil and even physical limitation.

I, too, have found that lending a hand can hold at bay that overwhelming urge to bolt from a meeting feeling unloved, unlovable, and forever being on the outside looking in. I, too, have found encouragement to let go of my isolation by replacing it with the conviction that *I can* make a contribution.

Practicing the Twelfth Step has given me a golden opportunity to look beyond my isolation and to begin following the guidance of a Higher Power in my daily life. When I look for what's wanted and needed at a meeting, I open the door to a deeper experience of using my will to do the will of a Higher Power. More time spent in the solution, no matter how brief a spell, inevitably allows for less time spent in the problem. Rather than reproducing the failure, resentment, and paralysis of dealing with the disease of alcoholism, Al-Anon service gives me a chance to step lightly into the fresh air of recovery. *I ask myself: Today, what time can I spend reaching out to others in recovery?*

Learning Trust

Practicing the Twelfth Step allows me to listen with compassion to the pain, bewilderment, and confusion of newcomers—without being paralyzed by my own despair. I can hear their overwhelming and difficult tales while still being aware that a Power greater than ourselves is available with solutions to problems we cannot solve. I can extend support and understanding with the thought that, perhaps for the first time in my life, I know where to turn for similar help. I've begun to act now with the confidence that, although my resources can be depleted, they can also be renewed.

When sharing my story in newcomers' meetings, I have

seen faces that showed pain and confusion begin to reflect hope. By explaining to others my sense of limitation in dealing with the disease of alcoholism, I have come to see my limits more clearly. By reassuring others that "there is no situation too difficult to be bettered and no unhappiness too great to be lessened," I am reminded repeatedly that these words apply to my own difficulties, too.

By talking to newcomers I realize that my most painful, destructive experiences with alcoholism have at last proved useful. Frustration, confusion, and despair have helped me to understand others and identify with their turmoil. Seeing new members apply Al-Anon principles reminds me that this program works, and that the guidance of a Higher Power can work miracles.

Participating in newcomers' meetings has also increased my sense of trust. Complete strangers have risked trusting me to introduce them to Al-Anon. By their action they have encouraged me to trust myself.

With help from the many newcomers I've introduced to this program, I've become more the person I really want to be. I've learned to lend a helping hand with the same sense of trust I feel when someone reaches out to me.

I ask myself: Am I willing to welcome newcomers to Al-Anon?

Being Willing

It's surprising, but I began doing service without knowing it. I had been experiencing a great deal of emotional pain in my marriage and was attending a beginners' meeting regularly. Because I really liked the woman then serving as our Group Representative, I made a point of arriving early to help her set up the room, the literature, and the coffee. This routine gave us time to talk. My motive for helping out was, in the beginning, purely selfish—which was okay, because that's what I needed.

Because I enjoyed the company of "winners," I volunteered to order literature for my other regular group. Going to the Literature Distribution Center to pick up my orders put me in contact with more people who were serious about their recovery. After two years in Al-Anon, I loved the improvement I saw in myself and decided to dive headfirst into service. I volunteered to be Group Representative for that first beginners' group and to keep our district's meeting list updated. In my third year in Al-Anon, I volunteered to co-chair the "Day of Workshops" for our district. I never had any doubts about my capabilities, because I'd been told repeatedly, "You don't have to be perfect—just willing."

I ask myself: Have I been involved in service without knowing it?

A Balanced Perspective

When I agreed to serve as Group Representative, I began attending district and Area Assembly meetings and bringing information back to my group. I'd accepted the position because another member had said that it provided an incredible opportunity to learn more about Al-Anon.

How right she was! Meeting with other Al-Anon members, I learned more about helping myself and my group to deal with the effects of alcoholism in our lives—and about reaching out to others affected by another's alcoholism but who were still unaware of Al-Anon.

And I learned more about myself. I started looking more honestly at my own behavior. In my "searching and fearless moral inventory," I discovered positive qualities worth developing, and I felt growing confidence and self-esteem.

I ask myself: Am I ready to learn something new about myself?

Lessons in Honesty

Over the years, I've had the privilege of sponsoring a number of people. Each one has contributed to my own recovery by providing insight into my behavior.

I learned, for example, that I couldn't take away another's pain. I could listen, share my experience, strength, and hope and then let go with a silent prayer. I didn't need to let others' problems consume my thoughts for hours.

Because I didn't have the heart to end a conversation, I had often spent hours on the phone. Gradually I set limits and learned to respect my own need for time. Making time for myself continues to be difficult, but whenever I do it, it becomes easier.

I've come to not take things personally. Many of those I sponsored came and went. Some were serious about building a relationship; others only seemed capable of lip service; still others outgrew me as their Sponsor and moved on. With each situation I came to realize that change was part of a growth process for me as well as for those I sponsored.

I've occasionally refused a member's request to sponsor them. As a human being with my own needs, I have limits to the time and energy I can devote to helping others. I can also recall the one and only time I had to terminate a sponsorship. It was because of my own pain—when sponsoring a woman experiencing the trauma of sexual abuse. The painful awareness of having been sexually abused myself interfered with my ability to support her.

Sponsorship has taught me so much. I've felt a love and closeness for every person I've sponsored, and I've come to understand there is no perfect method of sponsoring. Being nonjudgmental, flexible, and relaxed has helped me both to offer guidance and to be a better person myself.

I ask myself: Am I willing to grow through sponsorship?

Clearer Communication

I learned how to be a Sponsor by making mistakes. I knew that to sponsor an Al-Anon member meant to listen and to share my experience, strength, and hope. Still, I didn't know how to listen and truly hear, or how to share from my heart.

Through trial and error, I learned that my listening skills needed improvement. I needed the patience to hear the words and to ask for clarification on confusing topics. Sometimes I needed help to understand what was being said.

I learned that people are more willing and open to hear my response after I have listened to them without interruption. I learned to ask whether my response was wanted or if a suggestion about tools to apply to a problem would be welcome.

I learned the value of saying "I" instead of "you," to describe behavior by stating how I interpreted or perceived it. Now I often start by saying, "This is my perception and I may be wrong..." When I changed the way I shared my response, others could hear me out, whether they agreed with me or not.

Improved communication skills made a big difference in my relationships. Many problems worked themselves out when I cultivated my ability to listen. I show others how I wish to be treated through example—by how I treat them. I have been fortunate to be a Sponsor, and I believe it is my Higher Power's gentle way of helping me work on my program.

I ask myself: What might I learn from being a Sponsor?

Learning to Take Risks

When I was growing up, I often heard my mom say yes when she meant no. I concluded that, in order to preserve a friendship, I needed to do whatever someone else wanted. Al-Anon has taught me to make choices, to set limits, and sometimes to say no.

When it comes to service, I also have choices. I recall that when I said no to reading a piece of literature at a meeting, the no was accepted with love, and my self-esteem grew. Then came an opportunity to serve on a committee I really got excited about: for an Al-Anon dance. In high school I had always wanted to be part of the group that decorated for dances. Now was my chance.

The committee members treated me with love and acceptance while teaching me to hang crepe paper and to make three-dimensional designs. They reassured me I was doing well. My self-esteem blossomed and my self-confidence grew.

Today I still pick and choose when it comes to my Al-Anon participation. You won't find me answering the telephone at the information service or being a Group Representative, though I admire those who can do that which has no appeal for me. We each have special talents and individual gifts.

Working on an Al-Anon fund-raiser is one of the real joys in my life. Others patiently teach me new tasks. They love me when I make mistakes—and even when I don't! I don't have to be perfect to satisfy them. While learning to accept criticism offered with love, I've also learned to laugh at my mistakes and not take myself so seriously. All of these experiences have helped my self-esteem grow. Encouraged by the love and acceptance of others in the program, I look forward to participating in even more activities.

Service helps me stretch my boundaries. Taking risks helps me grow, and Al-Anon is a safe place to do just that: take a risk and grow. Now I can take on new projects at work and expand my career. The rewards of service have been worth the risks.

I ask myself: What are my special talents?

Increased Self-Esteem

Over seven years ago, very reluctantly, I moved to another state. I saw the move as another attempt at a geographic cure. It also meant living near my in-laws, many of whom are alcoholic. The move has turned out to be a great blessing, however, because here I discovered service.

Before the move, I'd been attending Al-Anon meetings for over a year, but our group had no links with other groups and no mention of service beyond the group. I had pitched in to clean up after meetings, but I hadn't noticed that my participation strengthened my recovery.

My new group was very different. I found the same love, acceptance, and understanding, but I also heard regularly about sponsorship and service. When an announcement was made that a district meeting was being held in a nearby town, I thought all Al-Anons in the district were supposed to attend, and I dutifully complied. How surprised I was to see only seven or eight people there—I'd expected 50 or 75! Someone explained that Group Representatives were supposed to attend and all others were welcome. My group's GR was happy to see another interested person, and she urged me to go with her to future meetings.

Next we attended an area assembly. This time I asked my GR what an assembly was and who attended. Before Al-Anon, having to know everything about everything had been a character defect. Now it became an asset. When I showed up at that assembly, my GR suggested I talk to our group about volunteering to serve as our Alternate GR, and I said I would. I guess she could see I needed the service more than the service needed me.

Six months later our GR moved and I became GR. For the past few years, I've tried my best to be a good representative—to mention at meetings how much service has helped me grow

and to encourage others who show an interest. Service has done more for my self-esteem than anything else in my life, and it has given me many Al-Anon friends all over the state.
I ask myself: Am I ready for new growth?

A Sense of Purpose

Participation in Al-Anon has helped me foster conditions in myself and others that encourage healing and growth. When I lend a hand setting up, cleaning up, or doing anything else, I support a program that has supported me. By giving something back, I give thanks for what I've received, and in giving thanks for what I've received, I make room to receive more.

I know now that my life has a purpose, and I can give thanks for this day. I can appreciate what one writer calls ordinary experience. I can imagine that sometimes in my day, whether I know it or not, I am doing God's will. That doesn't mean I need to do heroic acts, but that at any given time, emptying the waste-baskets or doing the dishes may be enough. (Smelling a rose may also be enough!) The thought that what I'm doing is enough is tremendously comforting to me: It definitely encourages me to feel a healthy sense of purpose.
I ask myself: How can I pass on the support I have received?

Making a Difference

When I started helping out in my group, I began to feel like I became a real part of it. I had a chance to talk to members who came a little early or stayed a little late. It was easier to ask questions about the Al-Anon program on a one-to-one basis. I soon volunteered to be the literature person and, later, Secretary. Each position increased my contact with other group members, who often shared their experience with me and enriched my understanding of how the program works.

As my confidence grew, I volunteered for Group Representative and then District Public Information Chairperson. My vision of the program broadened as its power grew in my daily life.

Being one of those hands in Al-Anon that reaches out when anyone needs help brings me deep satisfaction. I feel warm inside when a newcomer mentions finding Al-Anon through a booklet at a doctor's office, an Al-Anon speaker on a talk show, or a meeting reminder in our local newspaper. I may not have performed the action that carried the message, but I am part of the process that made the event happen. I know that I help our fellowship reach out to others, and I see myself as a valuable community member.

After feeling so powerless while living unsuccessfully with alcoholism, I see now that I can make a difference. I've learned to let go of the things I cannot change and to work on changing the things I can. I'm "letting it begin with me."

I ask myself: Am I ready to make a difference?

Paying a Debt

Years ago, Al-Anon gave me back my life. I continue to receive life-sustaining, life-enriching gifts by practicing the principles of this program. If somebody saved my life, I would feel indebted. Because Al-Anon is a fellowship, I feel indebted to every member. More important, I know intrinsically that I owe something to Al-Anon for all the experience, strength, and hope I've been given so freely and so joyously. A short conference with my Higher Power confirms my intuition, and I respond not in words but in actions.

There are many ways I can show my appreciation: make coffee; order literature for a group; write down my thoughts for possible publication; be a Group Representative or Area

Coordinator; put an extra dollar in the basket; answer the Information Service telephone and put up posters; deliver meeting schedules to facilities; introduce Al-Anon to professionals… I can, I can, I can! And I do.

Service is mine to do, when I can, where I can, what I can, all I can.

I ask myself: What gifts have I received from Al-Anon?

Reaching Out to Others

"Carrying the message." That's what I read on the wall at my first Al-Anon meeting more than five years ago. But how could I, so emotionally devastated by this disease of alcoholism, ever do this? I didn't know the message, and I thought the idea was crazy.

I found Al-Anon by accident. I knew all about drunks, but I didn't know about this program. Still, from my first meeting, I knew Al-Anon had something for me. I heard a promise of serenity and hope. Although I encountered tremendous resistance from the active alcoholics in my life, I held on.

The women in my group were not too sure what to make of me, a man who couldn't speak without crying, but they didn't laugh, and I kept coming back. After a while, with a lot of support, I didn't cry anymore. I started to grow.

I learned that I only had to *try* to carry the Al-Anon message to others and to practice its principles in all my affairs. To do this, I had to find a God of my understanding. Today that God is the love and peace of the program that grows in me one day at a time.

When I attend a meeting even though I'm late and don't feel like going, I've carried a message. When I stay afterward for a few minutes, I've carried a message. When I see that hurt look in a newcomer's eyes and I smile and say, "Hello," I've carried a message.

Today I no longer feel alone, and I carry the message that

the love and peace of this program reaches out to us all.
I ask myself: How can I "carry the message" today?

Learning to Care

It's been said that there is no abstract action. I reflect on this as I take out the trash and make a note of the housekeeping chore I'll tackle next. I know that life is not all work, but I have to work to keep my life in working order. More than that, my actions demonstrate what I care for in the world. When I do my chores, I show that I want to develop a deeper relationship with my wife. We love each other, and we have an easier time expressing love when our physical surrounding bear witness to attention and care. I take out the trash knowing I make the kitchen easier to work in. (It also encourages discussing subjects more enjoyable than trash.)

I adopt a similar point of view toward Al-Anon. I care about this program, and I do my best to put this caring into practice. I don't expect to receive recognition for my contribution; I'll receive satisfaction from knowing I've lent a helping hand. I'll know my action has aided an endeavor that benefits me enormously.

I've heard it said that we can do no great things, only little things with great heart. When I take out the trash, my action supports a relationship in which I feel great love. When I set out Al-Anon literature, type a telephone list, or simply welcome a newcomer standing alone after a meeting, I do a little thing with great heart. When I act on behalf of what I care about, I strengthen my ability to care. I reach out with the thankful realization that I am doing what others have done for me in the past—and with the confident expectation that, as I give to the world, the world will give to me.
I ask myself: What do I care about in Al-Anon?

A Lesson in Courage

I'm a shy person. When my Sponsor suggested volunteering for telephone service in our district, my first thought was, "I couldn't do that!" I've always found it hard to open up to others, and I've often felt intimidated by outgoing people. "Besides," I thought, "what could I possible have to say that could help someone?"

After some discussion with my Sponsor, I decided to take her suggestion and volunteer. I mainly gave callers a brief outline of the Al-Anon program and told them where the meetings were held.

After a few weeks of routine calls, however, I was awakened in the middle of the night by a call from a young woman who was very upset and angry. We talked a long time. At the end of the conversation she thanked me sincerely for my support, and I thanked her, too.

Before I went back to bed I prayed for this caller and thanked my Higher Power for giving me the words to help her.

The next week I happened to see the late-night caller at a meeting. I decided to approach her afterwards, even though I felt shy. When I introduced myself, she smiled and hugged me. She was glad to meet me, and we talked for a while. As I drove home, I realized my Higher Power had given me the courage to make the first effort at a friendship.

I was amazed that I'd helped her with a few encouraging words and a simple willingness to listen. Once again, I had let my Higher Power work through me.

I also understood what other Al-Anon members meant when they said, "To keep it, you have to give it away." Now I know the rewards of helping someone else without telling them what to do. Now whenever someone calls I say, "Thank you," because I feel glad to be helping with recovery, even in a small way. Discovering that I can do something to help has increased my confidence and self-esteem. For the little I have given, I have received a rich reward.

I ask myself: What can I say to help someone?

Learning to Do the Footwork

My grandfather, an avid gardener, used to tell a joke about a man showing a visitor through his garden. "Isn't it wonderful," exclaimed the guest, "what miracles God can work in a garden!" The gardener replied, "I just wish you'd seen it when God had it all to himself."

I think of my grandfather's story when I reflect on my progress in Al-Anon. I came to the program like a visitor to a garden, conscious of a healing benefit but unaware of the commitment of time and energy made by other members to produce this result. As I continued to attend meetings, I came to appreciate the contribution of those who maintained the consistency and clear focus of the program, but I didn't see myself as one of those people. After a while I became aware that I'd been a visitor at meetings long enough to understand how to participate not only as a member but also as a trusted servant. I'd progressed from being a visitor in someone else's garden to being a gardener myself.

Doing the chores that allow a group to flourish has given me a sense of purpose and coherence in other areas of my life as well. As I participate more in Al-Anon, I have a clearer sense of the progress that patience and commitment produce. As I join in maintaining a program that has spread around the world, I get a sense of hope for my own life's possibilities. I see a program that is the tangible result of members like myself doing footwork with a spiritual orientation, seeking to translate a Higher Power's guidance into practical action. Every meeting I attend is the flowering of many hours of service contributed by past and present Al-Anon members; every time I participate I reflect that this program of repetition, applied in all areas of my life, can provide me with a sense of guidance and connection that I would never have thought possible.

I've learned that a group's service positions aren't difficult or complex. The clear separation and limited responsibility of each shows the benefits of keeping it simple. Applying this notion has helped me maintain my peace of mind in all areas of my life.

Participation has also given me an unexpected benefit arising from the Al-Anon concept of rotation of leadership. If our tasks are clearly defined, they are also limited in duration. We depend on others in our fellowship for help. I discovered that sharing Al-Anon service has encouraged me to accept and even to seek help in other areas of my life as well. If I can lend a hand in helping others, others can do the same for me. Although I might not always get the help I want, I now feel much freer to ask, and I find myself more accepting of the help I receive.

Participating in service has not solved all my problems. Still, like the gardener, I now have a clearer picture than before of the footwork involved in supporting and cultivating the miracles of a Higher Power.

I ask myself: Where can I lend a hand?

A Lesson in Detachment

It wasn't too long after I began spending time at our Information Service Office answering the telephone and giving information about Al-Anon that I had my first really unexpected encounter with the rewards of service.

One afternoon a woman experiencing a great deal of confusion and pain walked into the office to talk about the alcoholic in her life. We talked for some time, and I shared what I could of my experience, strength, and hope. In the process, as I absorbed her pain, I also recalled my own encounters with alcoholism. I got upset myself.

Shortly after this troubled newcomer left the office, a member breezed in to fill a literature order. I felt a need to talk to him about my feelings. I don't recall clearly, but I think I mentioned how difficult it was to hear the turmoil of the woman who had just left, how concerned I was about whether I had helped her, and how drained I felt from the conversation.

In reply, he said he encouraged himself to feel that whatever effectiveness be brought to service was acceptable in the eyes of his Higher Power. Service was about encouraging his own recovery, and he gave himself permission to limit his activities to what felt challenging but not overwhelming. His attitude also conveyed that he didn't feel responsible for anyone else's recovery—not the woman's who preceded him in the office, and not mine.

I felt a weight lift from my shoulders. Apparently the God of my understanding was prompting me to let go of my own feelings of guilt and doubt about myself. It was not only possible, but also desirable and even healthy, to consider that I was not in charge of anyone's recovery. My words might have helped this woman in distress, or they might not have. I could certainly know that I wished her well, but I couldn't fix her life. I could do only a small part in recalling for both of us the hope of recovery—and in the eyes of my Higher Power, that's enough.

Mentally, I released this woman and her load of suffering. I turned my attention to a recovery in which I had more influence—my own. I asked the man leaving the office with his sack of literature if he would be my Sponsor, and he said yes. Since then, he has helped me to trust more fully in the God of my understanding.

I ask myself: What unexpected benefit have I received from service?

A Lesson in Acceptance

A recent brief encounter in service reminded me of the far-reaching benefits of practicing acceptance in my life. I answered a call to our Information Service from a man obviously agitated and confused wanting to attend his first Al-Anon meeting as soon as possible. He stated preferences for the location and makeup of the meeting that made it clear to me I had little in common with him—except, of course, the experience of having been affected by someone else's drinking.

While talking with the caller, I had a vivid realization that my personal reaction to his preferences was not affecting my response to his call for help. I accepted my internal reaction as valid for myself, and I accepted his particular requests as useful for guiding him to a meeting where he might feel most comfortable. More important, I accepted the fact that I was talking with a person feeling tremendous pain. While I haven't know the same circumstances he reported, I've known the turmoil resulting from them. Despite the superficial differences, I recognized his quandary. We shared a common bond: We had both been affected by someone else's drinking.

The effects of my brief encounter with this harried newcomer stuck with me and seemed to spill over into other areas of my life. I realized that responding to calls for Al-Anon information had increased my ability to listen to others and to stay focused on our common ground. Along with increased self-acceptance, I found common ground with acquaintances and coworkers more easily than usual. The conscious effort I'd made to practice acceptance during a two-minute telephone conversation had a far-reaching effect on the rest of my day.

I was able to focus on common tasks without being distracted by individual differences in personality or opinion. With gratitude, I noticed that those around me seemed to concentrate on simply doing the best they could without glorifying their successes of justifying their failures.

My encounter with this troubled newcomer was a good illustration of the way the rewards of service can spread into other areas of my life. A dash of acceptance, added through the grace of a Higher Power, can unexpectedly spread to color all aspects of life.

I ask myself: What lessons of service have I applied to my life?

Letting Go of Perfectionism

At the Al-Anon meeting I attend, members occasionally find reading the suggested format difficult. One might be distracted by confusion or pain. Another might be participating in what is a second, third, or (in one daunting case) even a fourth language. Another might have limited sight, understanding, or reading skills. And one member makes occasional reference to the "Serendipity Prayer"—a happy accident if ever there was one!

I find few events at a meeting more touching than the halting or confused delivery of these short texts that I usually take for granted. I find in these moments a poignant reminder that Al-Anon works at all levels of ability. If I compare my contribution to any other efforts, I hope to compare it only to my own past attempts. I look only for progress, not perfection. Increasingly, I see participation and service not as ways of perfecting my abilities or my knowledge, but as ways of learning to accept my imperfect performance.

In learning to accept my mistakes, I can better accept my own humanity, as well as that of others. While I can't achieve perfection, I can appreciate my own performance and the performances of those around me with a new sense of ease. In fact, with my more relaxed attitude I've also been able to achieve more than I truly value. My old desire for perfection tended to discourage me from taking any action at all, since it increased my own sense of dissatisfaction, inability, and failure. What I've discovered with the help of service in Al-Anon is that there is a wide range of results between perfect and ineffective, and that I can do much that brings me satisfaction and even joy.

Service has fostered a sense of ability and appreciation that replaces my old feelings of never being good enough. First, I have benefited greatly from the acceptance and appreciation of other members. They have consistently viewed my efforts as contributions to the group's welfare. I have yet to hear a suggestion that I study up on Al-Anon literature, improve my coffee-making skills, learn to direct meetings more smoothly, or brush up my treasury record keeping. Second, a sense of the acceptance and guidance of a Higher Power has encouraged me. I've been increasingly able to view my imperfect efforts as acceptable and well intentioned in the eyes of my Higher Power. While I grew up with the saying that the road to hell is paved with good intentions, I've learned more clearly through Al-Anon service that good intentions can also serve as the roadbed for many imperfect human acts of kindness, caring, and love.

I ask myself: What abilities have I learned to trust in Al-Anon?

Putting a Spiritual Awakening into Practice

One of the ways growing up in an alcoholic family has affected me is that I've had some difficulty in sticking up for myself. I've tended to discount my own sources of passion, enthusiasm, and interest as less worthy or valuable than those of others. The result: I spent a lot of time feeling confused and unhappy. In Al-Anon I've seen these feeling lift as I've begun to express myself. I've discovered that I have a voice, that I can make a contribution, that I can help support healing in the Al-Anon fellowship.

What I'm describing is my version of a spiritual awakening—a renewed sense of my own vitality and of the promise each day brings. With the help of a Power greater than myself, I now feel an appreciation for life.

The Twelfth Step suggests that I share this feeling with others, and I've done my best to do that. I have a few personal incentives for carrying the message of these Steps. First, there's the matter of personal honesty. I've received such a wealth of support, care, and wisdom from Al-Anon that I'd feel dishonest if I didn't share my experience with others.

My second incentive is simple: I want Al-Anon to continue to be available not only for others but also for me. I expect that there is still a certain amount of pain I'll encounter in this life, and I hope to face it with the support of this program.

My third incentive is more general. Carrying this message to others is the best way I know to express my thanks to those who carried this message to me. So many people have extended themselves generously to me. The truest form in which I can express my thanks is to learn to extend the same unselfish attention to others.

Last, but not least, carrying this message allows me to see my past in a more positive light. I can always be thankful that my past helps me listen to others with empathy, and that my story is not worse than it is.

To me the Twelfth Step is a practical way of sharing the benefits of recovery. I focus on moving beyond "talking the talk" to "walking the walk," with an understanding, as they say, that a journey of a thousand miles begins with a single step. I believe that actions speak much louder than words. With this step, I take action.

I ask myself: How have I put the Twelfth Step into action?

Learning to Say Yes

Occasionally at meetings I have heard the suggestion that we say yes to the program. While I haven't always said yes, I often have. While I have received great benefit by learning to say no and by learning that *no* is a complete sentence, I have also received great benefit from learning to say *yes* to service. *Yes* is just as complete a sentence as *no*, and in my experience, equally liberating when spoken without a sense of coercion, obligation, or hesitation.

Saying yes to service in the program has helped me learn to say yes to the rest of my life. More often than in my pre-Al-Anon days, I find myself responding to the spirit of these words quoted in our pamphlet, *Alcoholism, the Family Disease*: "Any good that I can do, or any kindness that I can show to any fellow creature, let me do it now. Let me not defer or neglect it, for I shall not pass this way again."

Saying yes to the program has taught me some discernment. I've learned more clearly that I have a choice every time I say yes. I've also learned that *yes* can be a specific response with limits. It is not a surrender of my capacity to make decisions. I can do *something* without being obliged to do *everything*.

In saying that I have learned some discernment, I mean also that saying yes to the program has given me a standard by which to gauge my choices. When I say yes to service, I usually have a positive experience. Now when a friend asks a favor or presents a plan, I have a clearer measure with which to gauge my response. Do I feel the sense of clear assent and confident anticipation that I feel when I say yes to the program? If so, I feel good about saying yes. If not, I say no.

I might add that I take time to deliberate. Not all opportunities are convenient, and I usually need time to consider the demands of my schedule and the details of my current needs.

In my life, as in Al-Anon, I've moved from being a fairly passive and dissatisfied observer to being a participant and an active contributor. Al-Anon service has given me the chance to realize that I have a life, that I have strong opinions, preferences, and values, and that I have the right to say yes to life on a daily basis in whatever way feels appropriate to me.

In service, I have learned to say yes to my life with discernment, clarity, and enthusiasm.

I ask myself: Do I say yes to the program?

Gratitude in Action

Some time ago I received from the World Service Office an informal photo of Lois W., cofounder of our program. When I want to get a clearer perspective on Al-Anon's origins and its place in my life, I look at my picture of Lois.

What I see in this woman's image is gratitude in action. I see Lois as an image of the many Al-Anon members from whom I have received the peace of this program—regular folks from all walks of life, people with no special credentials, degrees, certificates, titles, or privileges.

Each of them has done or said something from which I've gained a measure of serenity, courage, or wisdom. Each of them has striven to pass on a sense of a spiritual awakening with the same open-handed generosity extended to them. Each of them has helped me by acting on the thought that service is gratitude in action.

Lois' photo reminds me that I have much for which to give thanks and that I have an opportunity to give thanks in a very concrete way. Any and every service that I perform in Al-Anon holds an opportunity for me to acknowledge my gratitude and to practice the same generosity of spirit that I have so much appreciated in others.

The picture of Lois also provides me with reassurance. Lois had the common touch, she wore no halo, she achieved serenity through no special rigorous plan. She was guided by the same fallible human sense of inner light or Higher Power available to each of us, and she was satisfied with this condition. I feel reassured that today I can practice gratitude in action to the best of my ability, and that in doing so I can hope to experience more of the sense of confident expectation I believe I see in Lois. When I practice gratitude, I give proper thanks for all of the guidance I have received, and I try to cultivate the honesty, openness, and willingness that enable me to continue to receive it.

My picture of Lois also reminds me of a simple truth that I often overlook: Our program exists only because of the thousands of members like Lois who have been willing to serve others. Al-Anon is literally comprised of service: Without it, there would be no fellowship. Because no meeting takes place without it, service must be acknowledge as one of the cornerstones of Al-Anon. Every day that I attend a meeting or make contact with Al-Anon, I am benefiting from a long and continuous line of service extending back as far as Lois.

Isaac Newton said of his life and work that, if he had seen so far, it was "by standing on the shoulders of giants." Perhaps we in this program should adapt his reflection and acknowledge that, if in Al-Anon we have seen so far, it is because we have all stood on the shoulders of those who have prepared the way for us.

Participating in service has clearly demonstrated to me some of the day-to-day reality of recovery in Al-Anon stretching back over the last half-century; it has given me a sense that there is lasting hope in the world and that I can make a difference in preserving and imparting a continuing sense of positive achievement.

I see in my picture of Lois the presence of an inner light that she seems ready, willing, and able to share.

I ask myself: How have I made a difference today?

Learning to Love

I'm what's known as a dual member—both a recovering alcoholic and an Al-Anon member. For years I felt like a double loser. Not until I agreed to serve as an Alateen Group Sponsor did I begin to feel like a winner.

Before that, I had spent years in recovery trying to coax recovering alcoholics and Al-Anon members to understand and accept each other. In fact, I agreed to be an Alateen Group Sponsor because I thought I saw an opportunity to understand my son better. Before long, I discovered that the person benefiting most from my service wasn't my son but me.

To my surprise, I discovered that the crossfire in which I was caught was not a struggle between recovering alcoholics and their loved ones but between my two angry parents.

Participating in Alateen released me from my inner struggle to mediate for my parents. My lifelong role as embattled peacemaker in the crossfire ended. I learned to accept my parents' fights as theirs, not mine. I finally understood that my parents' inability to be civil to each other was not my responsibility.

In Alateen service I was encouraged to release my anger and self-pity about being raised in an alcoholic home with little or no security. I was able to admit for the first time that I loved my parents and that, though emotionally crippled, they loved me, too. This admission freed me to love *me*.

I no longer use my parents as a crutch or as an excuse for my failures, fears, and insecurities. Step by step, sponsoring an Alateen group gave me the courage to face each fear, to greet my life's challenges, and to develop my talents until that someone special in me became apparent even to me.

The final miracle I have received is that I have become capable of giving and receiving unconditional love. To my Higher Power and to the healing effects of my service in Alateen I am eternally grateful. They did for me what I could not do for myself.

I ask myself: How have I grown in service?

A Deeper Sense of a Higher Power

I used to see a member at our local information service office who put the Eleventh Step into action in service with surprising directness and simplicity. Before picking up the telephone to speak to a caller, he stopped momentarily to pray for the right words to say. I can't know how often his prayer was answered, but I feel certain it helped him choose his words with care. I'm sure this volunteer's prayer in service functioned in his own life as a practical reminder to continue to seek guidance through the course of his day.

Like him, I sense that, when I reach out to my Higher Power in Al-Anon, my Higher Power reaches back. I find new connections with individual members, and I have a renewed feeling of vitality. As if in a laboratory experiment, I receive clear and surprising confirmation that the care and commitment I put out to others comes back to me.

As I strive to do my Higher Power's will in service, I increasingly know that will more clearly. I feel an extended sense of balance in my daily affairs and a deepening tendency to accept more and judge less. I'm able to experience life more fully and to feel that more and more of what I do conforms to my Higher Power's will.

Albert Schweitzer said, "I don't know what your destiny will be, but one thing I do know: the only ones among you who will be really happy are those who have sought and found how to serve." In Al-Anon I have found the beginning of an answer for me. Service in this program has enlarged my understanding of my Higher Power's will and has started me on a course of lifelong learning.

I ask myself: Where have I found guidance in service?

Our Common Welfare

Service offers many of us a new experience in group participation. No longer isolated, we share a common welfare with
other Al-Anon members and also with people still seeking
help. A common bond unites us, despite our many differences.

As we reach out carrying Al-Anon's message of hope,
we look for confirmation that our actions in fact support our
common welfare. For guidance and support, we turn to the
Traditions and strive to practice our program's concept of
"obedience to the unenforceable." The Traditions offer guidance for our efforts, but we have individual responsibility for
applying them.

As we apply the Traditions to our actions, we notice that
these precepts for preserving unity can be applied to other
experiences and other relationships. Our families, friends,
business, and communities all provide fertile ground for practicing the principles of our Traditions, and as we do so, we
find ourselves growing by leaps and bounds.

•

**TRADITION ONE: Our common welfare should come
first; personal progress for the greatest number depends
upon unity.**

Reaching out in service gave me a new perspective on our
common welfare. My need for the support of the program
didn't end when I began carrying the message; I didn't gradu-

ate from bewildered student to serene, wise, and calm teacher. Instead, I felt a deeper acceptance of sharing a common problem with all Al-Anon members. In helping others, I was helping myself. When contributing to our common welfare, I was safeguarding my individual opportunity to make personal progress.

When joining with others in Al-Anon service, I also noticed that together we could accomplish what we couldn't achieve separately. We became more effective than the sum of our individual contributions. We helped each other to grow.

While service activity helped focus my attention on common welfare and unity, it didn't magically create a deeper sense of shared purpose in the rest of my life. It did, however, give me a basis of comparison for determining if a common welfare existed. Was unity a realistic goal in my dealings with family, friends, business, and community? Having applied the First Tradition to service in Al-Anon, I began to distinguish between relationships in which I participated in a common welfare and ones in which I didn't. I began to understand, as well, that when I felt no sense of unity with others, my personal welfare suffered.

●

TRADITION TWO: For our group purpose there is but one authority—a loving God as He may express Himself in our group conscience. Our leaders are but trusted servants—they do not govern.

When I began actively participating in my group, I noticed that other members responded to my efforts with encouragement and appreciation. No one insisted I arranged literature in a certain way, perform as Secretary with aplomb and clarity, or prepare the world's finest coffee. Members treated me gently not only out of courtesy, but also out of deference to the Second Tradition: I was functioning as a trusted servant, and no group member was attempting to assume authority by directing or controlling my efforts.

I began to lose my fear of criticism and to speak more easily in contributing to the group conscience. I, too, could take part in expressing the love of a Higher Power in the affairs of my group. I felt encouraged to cooperate as an equal with others.

In my life outside Al-Anon, I don't participate in many groups that even acknowledge a Higher Power as a presence in group activities, let alone recognize it as the sole authority. I do, however, participate in groups that operate on the basis of discussion, majority votes, and sometimes even consensus. In all these groups—and especially in my dealings with family and friends—I feel free to include my sense of a loving Higher Power in my personal deliberations. Sometimes, of course, this sense is stronger than others; my human ability to express the will of a Higher Power is limited. Even so, the guidance and encouragement of the Second Tradition have opened up avenues to participation that now extend well past my contributions in service.

●

TRADITION THREE: The relatives of alcoholics, when gathered together for mutual aid, may call themselves an Al-Anon Family Group, provided that, as a group, they have no other affiliation. The only requirement for membership is that there be a problem of alcoholism in a relative or friend.

In practicing the Twelfth Step, I've had many opportunities to refer to Tradition Three, usually to reassure a newcomer that the only membership requirement in Al-Anon is a problem with someone else's drinking. When I think of the millions of people worldwide who satisfy this single requirement, I understand very clearly just how inclusive Al-Anon is.

I've spoken also to a number of people (mostly by telephone) who are curious about Al-Anon but seem quite certain they haven't been affected by someone else's drinking. I've explained that Al-Anon has a requirement for membership and that it's up to the individual to decide how this requirement applies. I've also explained sometimes that Al-Anon is for people who have a problem with someone else's drinking rather than their own. I'm aware that we each judge for ourselves whether we may be able to benefit from Al-Anon. It's not unusual for individuals to come to our meetings and simply wonder if they belong. The awareness of the problems alcohol has brought to our lives sometimes comes slowly.

I've also occasionally come into contact with groups that call themselves Al-Anon Family Groups yet still have other affiliations. They had, you might say, overlooked the sole requirement for group membership. Again, I don't believe that Al-Anon needs gatekeepers, but in the spirit of Tradition One's appeal to our common welfare, I've done what I could to encourage our district to keep its focus on meetings that have no other affiliation.

My experience with this Tradition leads me to conclude that, while this program is inclusive, it has limits. It does not seek, and cannot manage, to be all things to all people. Within its focus, however, it includes all races, religions, and nationalities, all people without regard to external circumstances.

Honoring this Tradition in service has affected several areas of my life. In welcoming and reassuring Al-Anon newcomers, I focused on making them feel welcome, not on wondering if they belonged. In time I was able to consider that perhaps in other situations people might also honestly welcome me. Before this realization, I often felt too shy and insecure to venture into a group of people, no matter how desperately I wanted to join. Reassuring others new to the program that they qualify for membership has helped me reassure myself. Understanding that I really *do* belong in Al-Anon has helped me to see that, not only inside Al-Anon but outside as well, I don't need to complicate my life by trying to live up to special demanding conditions that I've invented for myself.

•

TRADITION FOUR: Each group should be autonomous, except in matters affecting another group or Al-Anon or AA as a whole.

When I began lending a hand in this program, I became more aware of taking part in the affairs of my group. With the realization that our group was an independent entity came an awareness that we also functioned cooperatively with other Al-Anon groups and with Al-Anon and A.A. as a whole. We were separate but not isolated. While we were responsible for conducting our meetings, we were asked to give primary consideration to the unity of Al-Anon as a whole.

While we functioned autonomously, we also functioned within the limits of the Twelve Traditions. We were free to operate as we liked, but within certain constraints.

In learning to apply the Fourth Tradition to the affairs of my group, I found two refreshing contrasts to the rules of the road that seemed to apply in my experience of dealing with alcoholism. First, the group limits to freedom of action were clear. We were trusted to run our group as we saw fit, except when our actions or decisions affected the unity of the fellowship or of A.A. As a group, we had freedom, but we did not have license. Second, we were encouraged to respect the limits of our autonomy, not through the harsh power of alcoholism, but through the gentle influence of a loving Higher Power.

As I gradually learned which matters affected other groups and the wider sphere of our fellowship and A.A., I came to think of my group as a cell in the body. We had an independent function, but we were part of a larger whole. We couldn't maintain a healthy independent function without fulfilling our function in the larger whole.

As I made efforts to support the dual awareness of an *independent group* contributing to the unity of a *larger whole*, I began to see parallels in other areas of my life. I was able to act with a more flexible awareness of freedom and responsibility. I became more adept at recognizing situations in which alcoholism or other problems conspired to set uncertain limits or to make punitive attempts at enforcement.

In my efforts to understand and apply Tradition Four's balance of freedom and responsibility, I've learned to adjust this balance in other areas of my life. With my family of origin, I've learned to take less responsibility; with my community, I've learned to take more. In both areas, I've relaxed my tendency to insist on functioning as a higher authority. I accept more readily the realization that the balance between freedom and responsibility is usually less well defined in other areas of my life than in Al-Anon. I give thanks for the welcome clarity of Tradition Four and do my best to apply its lesson in the limits of autonomy.

•

TRADITION FIVE: Each Al-Anon Family Group has but one purpose: to help families of alcoholics. We do this by practicing the Twelve Steps of AA *ourselves*, by encouraging and understanding our alcoholic relatives, and by welcoming and giving comfort to families of alcoholics.

I know an Al-Anon member who says firmly from time to time that Al-Anon is not a social club. Tradition Five reminds me that, unlike any sort of social club, my Al-Anon group's one purpose is to help families of alcoholics. This single clear group purpose frames all my efforts to reach out to others. In fact, it even extends the reach of my own efforts in recovery. I practice the Twelve Steps not only to help myself, but also to contribute to the group purpose. In seeking recovery for myself, I also make it available to the group.

Even in service, perhaps *especially* in service, I continue to keep my attention on weaving the Twelve Steps into the fabric of my life. Confusion, fear, faintheartedness, procrastination, self-will, and dominance all yield to the gentle influence of the Twelve Steps in service, as in the rest of my life. I cannot contribute to the group purpose unless I continue to practice the Steps with humility and faith. This practice, I believe, is the basis for being a trusted servant. To the best of my ability, I take the tools of the Twelve Steps with me when carrying the Al-Anon message. If I don't take care to bring my recovery with me, I cannot share it with others.

When reaching out to others, I sometimes have occasion to provide encouragement and understanding to alcoholics who are not my relatives. Sometime the understanding I need to practice is that not all members of A.A. realize that recovery in Al-Anon is distinct from recovery in A.A., and the encouragement I need to provide is the best example of practicing this program that I can embody.

Participation in Al-Anon Twelfth Step work has provided me with many opportunities to welcome and comfort newcomers. What makes this activity easier for me is the knowledge that I have a common experience with each of these people, regardless of external differences. While shyness might hold me back on the street, our group purpose gives me encouragement to extend my sense of recovery to newcomers.

The lessons of applying Tradition Five to service have extended dramatically into other areas of my life. Just as I've learned to take care to apply the Twelve Steps to my group experience, I've also learned to focus on using the Steps in other areas that I might have thought were beyond their reach. (Business comes to mind as an example.)

This Tradition has also helped me focus on a common purpose with others. I've learned to work more effectively on projects with others with whom I have differences by looking for common interests and working to achieve common goals.

Contributing to a group whose purpose is simple, clear, and positive has also helped me make progress in keeping other areas of my life simple, clear, and positive. Practicing these principles in Al-Anon encourages me to practice them in the rest of my life.

•

TRADITION SIX: Our Family Groups ought never endorse, finance or lend our name to any outside enterprise, lest problems of money, property and prestige divert us from our primary spiritual aim. Although a separate entity, we should always co-operate with Alcoholics Anonymous.

Active participation has given me new opportunities to appreciate aspects of Al-Anon that I tend to overlook. Tradition Six is a case in point. When I first came to Al-Anon, I didn't give much thought to the clear focus of the groups. I simply did my best to apply the Twelve Steps and the slogans to my own problems. Only later did I come to understand the role an undiverted group focus played in my personal recovery. With the passage of time, I realized that only if my group kept the focus on our program could I hope to do the same.

When taking part in service, I also benefited, at first unwittingly, from Tradition Six. As a literature volunteer, my responsibility was to replenish our stock of Al-Anon literature; I didn't need to concern myself with evaluating or purchasing other literature on alcoholism. As a Treasurer, I didn't need to concern myself with requests for contributions to other groups or organizations. As a Secretary, I didn't need to direct any debates about outside groups. And as Group Representative, I was concerned only with learning about the affairs of Al-Anon. For the most part, this Tradition worked so well that I benefited from it without giving it much attention.

In all my years in Al-Anon, I've yet to see a group consider supporting any outside enterprise. For the simplicity this Tradition has encouraged in carrying the Al-Anon message, as well as in working other aspects of my program, I give thanks.

Through Twelfth Step activities, I also have an extended awareness of the usefulness of this Tradition. Even within Al-Anon I've certainly found that problems of money, property, and prestige can crop up, and that they tend to divert us from our primary spiritual aim. In service, I've found the need to do my best to redirect my attention to our primary spiritual aim when I've found it wandering. When I'm diverted from this aim, I feel that I'm supporting neither my own recovery nor that of the fellowship.

I've learned to apply Tradition Six to my life outside of Al-Anon as well. I'm reminded that, in recovery, I feel that all of my existence has a primary spiritual aim. When I succeed in simplifying my life to include fewer problems of money, property, and prestige, I encourage myself to focus more clearly on my spiritual experience.

•

TRADITION SEVEN: Every group ought to be fully self-supporting, declining outside contributions.

My efforts to share the program have been kept clearer and simpler through the universal observance of Tradition Seven. I've never encountered an Al-Anon group that accepted financial contributions from outsiders. As a result, I've never heard a discussion in which any individual or group was mentioned as contributing to the well-being of any Al-Anon group. I've always felt certain that the funds available for any group's Twelfth Step activities were contributed by group members, and that my participation in Al-Anon service was funded only by group donations. I've always understood that we depended on one another to be self-supporting.

I've felt my own self-esteem and confidence grow as I've spent time functioning in a group that supports its own efforts. I take satisfaction in observing that our contributions enable us to rent the room where we meet, to purchase the literature we display, and to support the services of Al-Anon in our district, our Area, and around the world. In service, I've begun to see more clearly where our contributions go. As Treasurer, I have written the checks for our materials and for Twelfth Step work. As Information Service volunteer, I've seen the office from which our district responds to Twelfth Step calls. As Secretary, I've seen the newsletters and information we receive from our Area and World Service.

The group's willingness to observe the Seventh Tradition has literally made it possible for me to participate in service and to take pride in our contribution to recovery here and around the world. I feel a real debt of gratitude to all Al-Anon members who have kept our fellowship self-supporting over the years.

In service, I've not only benefited from the responsible and continuous practice of the Seventh Tradition, but I've also come to a wider understanding of its implications. While being fully self-supporting begins with declining outside contributions, it doesn't end there. Without the willingness to contribute time and energy as well, we can't succeed in observing the spirit of this Tradition. A group without trusted servants couldn't really be thought of as self-supporting. In service, then, I've realized a new dimension to being self-supporting. My group survives not only through its members' financial contributions, but also through their contributions of time and energy. In reference to Tradition Seven, our concept of "obedience to the unenforceable" encourages me to step forward and learn a lesson in fuller participation and greater self-esteem.

Participation in a group whose ideal is to be fully self-supporting carriers over into other areas of my life. While it's an understatement bordering on the laughable, it's nevertheless true that alcoholism has not been kind in providing me with friends and family willing and able to be fully self-supporting. Even those with plenty of money have been hard pressed to function responsibly. My Al-Anon service experience has encouraged me to learn more fully what it means to care for myself—not just financially but physically, emotionally, and spiritually. It has also taught me that, while I can contribute to a groups' well-being, I must also look to others in the group to take part.

•

TRADITION EIGHT: Al-Anon Twelfth Step work should remain forever non-professional, but our service centers may employ special workers.

Indirectly, Tradition Eight tells me one of the most important pieces of information I need to know about service in Al-Anon: By simply working the program, I am qualified to assume any service position in it. I don't need special training, just a willingness to carry the message.

As always in Al-Anon, I have found that I'm not alone. Many experienced members have helped me learn unfamiliar tasks.

Spending some time in the program is a suggested prerequisite for certain positions. No amount of time, however, makes us certified experts in Al-Anon, and none of us earns a special credential. Absorbing the principles of the program takes time, but we're free to do so just as we work all aspects of Al-Anon—in our own way and at our own pace.

Tradition Eight assures me that my invitation to service will always be open. The work we do to carry the message will always be performed by Al-Anon members sharing experience, strength, and hope, regardless of their professional background or training. My experience in dealing with alcoholism by using tools of the Al-Anon program is the only necessary reference point for Twelfth Step work, and this will never change. I can always be certain that I'm qualified, always feel sure that my experience in dealing with alcoholism can be useful, regardless of my particular story.

Tradition Eight also suggests one special satisfaction of service. Not only do I carry the Al-Anon message; I also help prepare those to whom I carry it for their eventual participation in practicing the Twelfth Step themselves. I carry this message of hope with the confident expectation that others will also want to carry it—and with the clear understanding that no one but Al-Anon members can take responsibility for the program's continuing vitality. Members to whom I carry the message may be the very same people who share their experience with me tomorrow. We all contribute in unique ways to make Al-Anon a source of common strength greater than the sum of its members.

Tradition Eight has encouraged me to try service, and it has also helped broaden my horizons in other areas. I've come to think of myself not as a person with limited professional expertise, but as a person with many unclassified but useful abilities. Just as I've found that my most painful and frustrating experiences in dealing with alcoholism have given me a useful common ground with others in Al-Anon, I've found that other overlooked experiences have proved to be sources of comfort and guidance in various areas of life. My past mistakes don't disqualify me from participating, but provide me instead with a basis for improvement. I feel a new confidence that who I am and what I have to give can be useful in the world.

●

TRADITION NINE: Our groups, as such, ought never be organized; but we may create service boards or committees directly responsible to those they serve.

Tradition Nine helps me with one of the most difficult facets of my life. Power and control—or, as it is described in the pamphlet, *Alcoholism, the Family Disease,* dominance. This Tradition clearly identifies the group as the primary focus of our collective efforts in service, and it suggests the limitations of any service I many perform. I am not asked to take over any aspect of my group, and I don't *become* a Secretary or Treasurer. I simply take on a limited responsibility for a limited length of time and serve the group to the best of my ability. I am not encouraged to identify myself with any of the roles I try on, and I am encouraged to pass the job on after a fairly definite period of time. Al-Anon calls this arrangement "rotation of leadership," and I find in this concept the encouragement to participate without exerting control and to let go without worrying that others might not step forward to carry on.

Tradition Nine also helps me join in without getting caught up in competition and perfectionism. I can feel confident that almost any type of service I want to try will sooner or later be available to me. In any task I do try, I can reassure myself that I am not obliged to live up to anyone else's standards, because no one holds any kind of authority in our groups. I face no performance review board or job evaluation committee.

My experience with service and Tradition Nine has helped me in the rest of my life. I've come to realize that I've often looked for groups that were highly organized because I thought such groups were more effective. I see now that they simply spent a lot of energy maintaining a high level of control. In a group with a common purpose, the common interest of the members can accomplish much without engaging in exhausting battles over control. In my struggles with the effects of alcoholism, I though that the only alternative to strict organization was chaos; I am learning that there is a middle ground between the two—cooperation.

•

TRADITION TEN: The Al-Anon Family Groups have no opinion on outside issues; hence our name ought never be drawn into public controversy.

I know an Al-Anon member who is careful to preface her expressions of opinion by saying, "This is my opinion and my opinion only." Her attention to stating her opinion without affiliating herself with any larger group or higher authority allows her to speak her mind freely and clearly without antagonizing others. I also detect in her approach the influence of our Tenth Tradition. She does not presume to speak for Al-Anon, and she does not present her opinions in the context of Al-Anon meetings.

The Tenth Tradition, of course, does more than encourage me to identify opinions I express as my own. It safeguards the program by avoiding public controversy. This Tradition contains no exceptions, no instances in which I may represent the program in any sort of public discussion of outside issues.

My experience in service has benefited greatly from this Tradition. I've never been confused by having to decide what Al-Anon stood for and whether I supported this or that position. I've never felt that my efforts were being directed to any cause except the recovery of Al-Anon members. I've also never felt a responsibility to defend Al-Anon itself from public comment about it. Even the public opinions of others about this program can be thought of as outside issues. I *do* care what others think of Al-Anon, and I *do* strive to embody the principles of the program, but I haven't found that the effectiveness of the program is in any way affected by public debate about the nature of alcoholism and recovery. We best serve our purpose by focusing clearly on helping those who want help.

Service has given me the opportunity to realize that Al-Anon has succeeded in avoiding public controversy by avoiding outside issues. I have benefited by realizing that, in other areas of my life, I am not obliged to hold or express opinions. While I do wish to lead a life that has principle and a positive effect, I need not feel it necessary to express an opinion in a situation where the resulting discussion, disagreement, or controversy will simply heighten antagonism between myself and another person. I need not engage in a discussion simply to avoid silence, and I need not conclude that, if I have no opinion on a subject, I've forfeited my ability to lead a responsible life.

Before Al-Anon, I sometimes expressed strong opinions out of fear of admitting I might be confused or uncertain. Since entering the program, I've used the experience of applying Tradition Ten to service in order to realize that I often make better progress when I avoid the distractions of controversy.

•

TRADITION ELEVEN: Our public relations policy is based on attraction rather than promotion; we need always maintain personal anonymity at the level of press, radio, films, and TV. We need guard with special care the anonymity of all AA members.

Tradition Eleven has provided great encouragement for me in practicing the Twelfth Step. Before Al-Anon, I was involved in a group in which promotion was the basis of all public relations. Not only was I ill-equipped to support intensive promotional activities, but I also found myself uncomfortable with the practice of persuading others to participate in activities that they might not be convinced were helpful.

In sharing Al-Anon with newcomers, I've done my best to extend a welcoming hand with the clear understanding that I wanted to offer encouragement—but no pressure—to join the program. I've seen many members find guidance in Al-Anon—but, as one longtimer puts it, "nothing is for everyone." Practicing the Twelfth Step has never put me in a position of having to do more than simply share my experience, strength, and hope. I do this not only by sharing about myself, but by putting Al-Anon literature where it might be seen by, and attract, others.

The reassuring experience of applying the guidelines of the Eleventh Tradition to service has helped me outside Al-Anon, too. I have seen that "attraction rather than promotion" is a viable practice in other areas of my life. When I do good work, I find now that it is often noticed and appreciated. I also find that friends and acquaintances who enter my life through attraction remain more vital than those who appear through events and activities that are more like promotion.

Although in Al-Anon I have had no personal opportunity to practice anonymity at the level of press, radio, films, and TV, I understand this suggestion as an extension of the concept of attraction rather than promotion. None of us speaks as the voice of Al-Anon; none of us is encouraged to use our personality to focus attention on the program; and each of us has the damaging power to undermine Al-Anon's spiritual foundation by breaking our anonymity at the public level.

Certainly I have seen anonymity at the public level breached with increasing frequency, and I have noticed my own tendency to identify those breaking their anonymity as somehow personally representative of the program.

This Tradition's emphasis on public anonymity *does* help to remind me that my goal in Al-Anon service is not to achieve recognition for myself, but rather to carry Al-Anon's message of recovery. The humility learned in practicing the Twelve Steps must accompany my efforts to reach out to others. As the book, *Al-Anon's Twelve Steps & Twelve Traditions* says, "Service makes us all equals."

•

TRADITION TWELVE: Anonymity is the spiritual foundation of all our Traditions, ever reminding us to place principles above personalities.

When I first came to Al-Anon, I was encouraged to leave the particulars of my individual identity at the door. I felt relieved to be able to focus on the effects of the disease of alcoholism in my life without reference to the details of my daily life. For my own reasons, I didn't feel particularly comfortable with myself and I was happy to be able to talk about my experience without feeling that anyone else was trying to intrude into my personal affairs. From this early encounter with the principle of anonymity, I began to get a feeling that other Al-Anon members truly believed in supporting my right to the dignity of making my own decisions.

I apparently had equal access to the wisdom and understanding that other members seemed to share so freely, regardless of who I was, what I had done or failed to do, where I had come from, or where I might be going. To me it seemed that perhaps the Higher Power saw each of us, in all our individual differences, as equally valuable. I began to feel encouraged to act as an equal member of each of the Al-Anon groups that I attended.

My growing sense of safety, acceptance, and full equality

made it much easier for me to try service. In all of the efforts I made, I found the support and guidance I needed to do what needed to be done. I began to feel able to extend to others the respect without reference to individual differences that had been extended to me.

Being human, I also discovered that focusing on the principles of the program was more difficult with some personalities than with others. The true worth of Tradition Twelve has emerged in my dealings with those members I find difficult or challenging, since it is most apparent in these situations that what unites us is not personalities but principles. When I remind myself to focus on the principles of the program, I find the guidance I need to deal with the personalities—mine as well as others'.

Learning to place principles above personalities in service has helped me with many other phases of my life. I have more success in seeing myself on an equal footing with others, regardless of their status, and I'm more effective at treating myself and others with care. I also feel less inclined to blame others for my problems.

Applying Tradition Twelve in service has given me encouragement to establish a spiritual foundation in many areas of my life.

Reaching Out to Others

In reaching out to others through Al-Anon service, we have the opportunity to share our unique experience and our personal recovery for a common good. We have the chance to encourage detachment, acceptance, and serenity in a supportive environment and to get to know ourselves better—both strengths and weakness—in the process.

We have the opportunity to contribute not only what we

can *do* but, more important, who we can *be*. By sharing our recovery, we strengthen its workings in our own lives. By seeking to allow a Higher Power to work in and through us, we come to feel, more fully, the presence of that Power.

In giving, we receive.

Twelve Steps

1. We admitted we were powerless over alcohol—that our lives had become unmanageable.
2. Came to believe that a Power greater than ourselves could restore us to sanity.
3. Made a decision to turn our will and our lives over to the care of God *as we understood Him.*
4. Made a searching and fearless moral inventory of ourselves.
5. Admitted to God, to ourselves, and to another human being the exact nature of our wrongs.
6. Were entirely ready to have God remove all these defects of character.
7. Humbly asked Him to remove our shortcomings.
8. Made a list of all persons we had harmed, and became willing to make amends to them all.
9. Made direct amends to such people wherever possible, except when to do so would injure them or others.
10. Continued to take personal inventory and when we were wrong promptly admitted it.
11. Sought through prayer and meditation to improve our conscious contact with God *as we understood Him,* praying only for knowledge of His will for us and the power to carry that out.
12. Having had a spiritual awakening as the result of these steps, we tried to carry this message to others, and to practice these principles in all our affairs.

Index